WOMEN'S PERSPECTIVES

Gospel and Culture pamphlets:

1. S. Wesley Ariarajah, *An Ongoing Discussion in the Ecumenical Movement*
2. Stan McKay and Janet Silman, *The First Nations of Canada*
3. Ion Bria, *Romania*
4. Noel Davies, *Wales*
5. James Massey, *Panjab*
6. Antonie Wessels, *Secularized Europe*
7. Israel Selvanayagam, *Tamilnadu*
8. Ambrose Moyo, *Zimbabwe*
9. John Pobee, *West Africa*
10. Lewin L. Williams, *The Caribbean*
11. Donald E. Meek, *The Scottish Highlands*
12. Allan K. Davidson, *Aotearoa New Zealand*
13. *Germany*
14. *Women's Perspectives*
15. K.M. George, *The Early Church*

GOSPEL AND CULTURES PAMPHLET 14

WOMEN'S PERSPECTIVES

*Articulating the
Liberating Power of the Gospel*

Seven essays

WCC Publications, Geneva

Cover design: Edwin Hassink
Cover illustration: The logo of the Decade Festival in 1998, by Eva Saro. The Festival will bring together women from around the world to mark the end of the World Council of Churches' Ecumenical Decade of Churches in Solidarity with Women. It will celebrate the lives and contributions of women to church and society, articulate women's visions and undertake new commitments for fuller life for all. This booklet is a contribution to the preparatory process for the Decade Festival.

ISBN 2-8254-1208-2

© 1996 WCC Publications, World Council of Churches,
150 route de Ferney, 1211 Geneva 2, Switzerland

No. 14 in the Gospel and Cultures Series

Printed in Switzerland

Table of Contents

vii   INTRODUCTION   *Jean Stromberg*

1   1. THE SILENCE OF WOMEN
       Bärbel von Wartenberg-Potter

7   2. A *MUJERISTA* PERSPECTIVE ON GOSPEL
       AND CULTURE   *Ada Maria Isasi-Diaz*

14   3. GOSPEL, CULTURE AND WOMEN IN AN
       AFRICAN-AMERICAN CONTEXT
       Delores S. Williams

23   4. REREADING THE BIBLE AS A LATIN AMERICAN
       BLACK WOMAN   *Silvia Regina de Lima*

28   5. THE WISDOM OF MOTHERS KNOWS
       NO BOUNDARIES   *Chung Hyun-Kyung*

36   6. GOSPEL AND CULTURES IN AFRICA: THROUGH
       WOMEN'S EYES   *Mercy Amba Oduyoye*

48   7. "SEEING THE WORLD THROUGH
       WOMEN'S EYES"   *Ofelia Ortega*

52   CONTRIBUTORS

Introduction

JEAN STROMBERG

"Culture shapes the human voice that answers the voice of Christ."[1] If the voice that answers Christ is a woman's voice, how has it been shaped by the culture in which that woman lives? How has the voice of Christ been heard by women in cultures around the world?

The forum for nongovernmental organizations which met in Huairou, China, in connection with the United Nations' Fourth World Conference on Women in Beijing in August 1995 provided a global opportunity for the World Council of Churches to pursue its reflection on gospel and cultures with and by women from various parts of the world. The WCC organized two workshops in Huairou to explore the relationship of religious faith and cultures: "Women, Religion and Cultures — Christian Perspectives" and "Gospel, Cultures and Women". The response was enthusiastic. Participants crowded the assigned rooms and engaged in animated discussions following the presentations. We hope that readers of this pamphlet, which brings together presentations from those workshops, will be helped to discover how women are hearing and living the gospel in different cultural contexts.

While religion has often been accused of contributing to the oppression of women, it came as a surprise for Christian women who have been at the cutting edge of women's issues within the churches and have even suffered because of their stand to find that women of faith were not always welcomed within the wider expressions of the women's movement at the NGO forum.

Most references to religion were linked to fundamentalism and conservatism. In a plenary I attended, the speaker stated, without nuances, that religious identity feeds conservatism and the oppression of women. Yet while it was discouraging to see this sidelining of the contribution of women of faith, the NGO forum points both to the need and the challenge to Christian women to articulate the liberating power of the gospel in words that can be heard by others today.

The Christian women present in Huairou fully recognized and have indeed suffered under the oppression imposed by various church structures, theological constructs or biblical interpretations. Nevertheless, they asserted, there are stories of hope to be shared. Christian women's analysis of the problems women face may be similar to others', and their solidarity may seek similar solutions; but the experience of the liberating power of the gospel and the hope found in God's promises are unique gifts which Christian women bring to the human community.

In her contribution, Bärbel von Wartenberg-Potter lifts up one element of women's heritage which might be viewed as part of the oppression: the silence of women. That this silence is being overcome, as well as used in subversive ways, is part of the hope to which women of faith may point. She calls women to use their voice "for the sake of a better world in which God's love can be experienced by all God's creatures".

The experience of Huairou adds urgency to the call to women to use their voices to tell stories of where God's liberating love is in fact being experienced. As von Wartenberg-Potter reminds us, women were the first to bring the resurrection news to the sceptical disciples; Christian women today must speak their witness to the "power of life over death, the power which changes history" to a world which increasingly discounts religious faith.

Affirming discoveries

What are the discoveries of women as they respond to the call of the gospel from within their particular cultural context? Four basic affirmations emerge from the workshops.

1. The gospel is liberating. In these presentations the clarity of the gospel is striking. The gospel is good news — life-giving, liberating, energizing! It is dynamic and alive, a source of strength and power. Its values, according to Ada Maria Isasi-Diaz, are community, justice and shalom.

This may sound deceptively simple, until one considers how often the gospel has been heard as something other than good news, especially for women. This is no less than a call to the difficult work of hearing and articulating the gospel anew.

Delores Williams shows how the gospel which slaveholders brought to slaves had to be reinterpreted to be the gospel. When over time, doctrine and male dominance made that retelling oppressive, another retelling by women was called for.

This rereading of the Bible, Sylvia Regina de Lima points out, demands a series of breaks with tradition, even to the point of liberating God from the narrow concepts to which God was reduced by Western Christianity.

Women today are articulating the liberating message of the gospel in ways that correspond to their own cultural context. These responses are radically different from expressions of the gospel that arose out of quite different experiences. Will they be heard? Will they be allowed to enrich the whole Christian community?

2. *The relationship between the gospel and culture is complex and multifaceted.* Among the missionaries of the past who promoted a sense of Western cultural superiority were many women. It is therefore appropriate that some of the strongest voices today exploring the frontiers of the gospel-culture relationship are women who have encountered that legacy. Chung Hyun-Kyung challenges not only the colonial heritage of superiority, but any model in which the gospel and Christ are always connected with seed or yeast and cultures and religions are considered as soil or dough. Isasi-Diaz argues that culture is basically how humans construct reality; therefore women are encouraged to change constructed reality when it does not correspond to the life-giving gospel.

The gospel critique of cultures which maintain or promote that which oppresses or devalues women is clear. What may be less clear to many women is how to discover the gospel in daily lives that have been discounted by cultures. Here we can learn from other women that God "communicates with us in the rhythm of our daily lives, orchestrated by the instruments of our various cultures" (Williams). For black women in Latin America, there is a connectedness that finds "God-experience in the form of succour in time of need. God is health in the form of blessing, herbal teas and baths...; food that is shared on feast days or with a neighbour in times of need" (Regina de Lima).

Mercy Amba Oduyoye goes beyond juxtaposing gospel and cultures to a critical appropriation of both the received culture and the received religion in her proposal for a "gospel culture: a way of life creatively crafted from the humanizing elements of our cultures". Such a gospel culture would challenge both church and society for trivializing the humanity of women.

All the workshop contributions wrestle in one way or another with an integral relationship that pushes beyond easy categorizations. Are there insights here, springing from the daily lives of women, which will facilitate new understandings and expressions of this complex relationship?

3. Pluralism is the way it is. If God's love, revealed in Jesus Christ, shows itself in particular contexts and through particular cultures, Christian women living out our faith are challenged to be a rich mosaic, a "multidimensional variegated beauty that we can celebrate together", rather than something monolithic.

Two specific challenges emerge. The first is that pluralism is not "neat". "Clear" pluralism exists only in academia, according to Chung. As several of the contributions point out, pluralism is often within women's own lives; they encounter it in the search for their own identities. The second challenge is to deal with differences. We have gone too quickly from ignoring differences to celebrating differences. According to Isasi-Diaz, we need to engage our differences, which will involve the challenge of rejecting "essentialism" and clarifying together the values we can agree on.

Can we as women play a particular role in enabling various cultural expressions of Christian faith to be in dialogue with each other? Are our identities as women more important than our identity as children of God? Where does the search for our own identity become separatist and destructive? This poses an especially difficult challenge to minority ethnic women.

4. We need each other as women in community. The workshops in Huairou were rich experiences of sharing women's experiences from every part of our globe. These presentations freely acknowledge the gifts of wisdom and strength received from other women; they inspire women everywhere to find ways to reach out to each other across barriers of time, language and space. When women read the Bible together, the stories are heard differently; when women share stories of hope, other women see more clearly how they too may hope. Women who have experienced invisibility will not let other women remain invisible. Women whose voices have been drowned out will be sensitive to women who are voiceless.

We need each other in community. The sense of community revealed in these presentations enlarges, for many of us, the scope and meaning of community. This community reaches into time to include both the living and the dead. It reaches into the space around us to include nature. It is God who makes this community and brings us into communion with all around us. It is in this community that we become persons. In this community there is respect for the other and for the environment.

Will women be able lead the way in transcending the competitiveness and individualism of many cultural contexts? In overcoming rigid understandings of the feminine and masculine in the building of community?

* * *

In the presentations here, we enter into an exciting discussion of the relationship of gospel and cultures from the perspectives of women. As the global study process continues, we invite and anticipate the significant role that women will play in enabling the whole Christian family to hear the gospel anew, in deepening the understanding of the multifaceted relationship of gospel and cultures and in affirming the rich plurality with which God has blessed our world.

Oduyoye asks: "What is the vision of a community that lives as though God is indeed with us?"

Among the voices that answer that question must be those of women, who offer unique contributions out of the concreteness of their lives, out of the poverty in which so many live, out of their intimate contact with the most vulnerable in their societies, out of their deepest reflections and experience with life. Women's voices are critical in the assessment of what is truly liberating and life-giving in the human community, what is authentic witness to the gospel today.

NOTE

[1] From the report of section 2, "Culture and Identity", at the WCC's world mission conference in Bangkok, 1972-73; *Bangkok Assembly 1973*, Geneva, WCC, 1973, p.73.

1. The Silence of Women

BÄRBEL VON WARTENBERG-POTTER

Religion and culture have often been identified as chief contributors to the oppression of women by maintaining traditions which denigrate women and deny them equal rights and opportunities. As women of faith we take this accusation very seriously. Our task is to challenge everything in our religious tradition that denies women their rights as human beings created in God's image and likeness. The world and our faith communities need the gifts of women. We cannot afford to leave the world in the hands of men alone. Too often male domination has brought the world to the brink of an abyss. Together we want to take responsibility and develop all our God-given gifts in equality — for the sake of the well-being of the whole human family.

Silence of women — enforced by religion and culture

One heritage which has been ours over many centuries, which we share with women of other faiths and other cultures, is the religiously imposed and sanctioned silence of women. This has been forced on women in manifold ways. Rabbis, mullahs, priests, popes, patriarchs, bishops and other religious leaders of different traditions have this in common: to this very day, most do not allow women access to writing and teaching and especially to officiating at religious practices and services.

A powerful means to prevent the equal sharing of spiritual and theological gifts is the imposition of silence on women and about women. Women have been taught and forced to keep silent in the realms of public pronouncements and the relation of religious experiences. Religious texts and traditions have legitimized and enforced this silence. It surrounds women's lives. The apostle Paul writes: "I permit no woman to teach or to have authority over a man; she is to keep silent" (1 Tim. 2:12). In the First Letter to Corinthians we read: "As in all the churches of the saints, women should be silent in the churches. For they are not permitted to speak, but should be subordinate, as the law also says. If there is anything they desire to know, let them ask their husbands at home. For it is shameful for a woman to speak in church" (1 Cor. 14:34-35).

In my own German culture there used to be many rules which a well-educated girl or woman had to keep. She did not speak in public. She listened to what others said. She pleased her husband and family with decent conduct. She kept her thoughts in her heart. She did not question the decisions of her father or husband. To learn these rules was part of a girl's education.

Today women in almost all cultures have broken the spell of silence which covers women's lives and her-story. But many girls and women have internalized the rules of "decent conduct". Religious institutions still keep women out.

Today we remember the silence of our ancestors, mothers and grandmothers. They kept silent
— about the experiences in a woman's life: about growing up as a girl, first menstruation, awakening sexuality, childbearing and birth, menopause and ageing, women loving women;
— about violence against women, about child abuse, the early mutilation of women's bodies, binding feet, female circumcision, rape and wife-beating, murder of unwanted female babies;
— about pains and injustices and the neglect of women in daily life, in refugee camps and in rural fields, about women's health, about labour conditions, child labour, unequal pay, and sexual harassment;
— about spiritual insights, their stories with God and with each other, what sustains their lives, the crosses they bear, the power of the Holy in their lives.

Silencing was a means of oppressing women or trivializing their experiences, of not allowing them to express their innermost thoughts about what moves and sustains them.

Silence as power

Women on their way to emancipation have not simply thrown off this silence. Why not? Because women have cleverly used silence as a powerful means to communicate. Where oppression could not be overcome with words, women have turned the imposed silence into instruments of their own power.

The first time I experienced the power of silent demonstration was in Argentina when I saw the Mothers of the Plaza de Mayo. Every week they marched around the central square in Buenos Aires with pictures of their loved ones who had "disappeared". With this silent demonstration they unmasked before the eyes of the world the injustices of the military dictatorship.

This practice has been taken up by countless women in many places in the world: women in black in Jerusalem and the former Yugoslavia; women in silent vigils in the era of apartheid in South Africa. Candlelight vigils in East Germany were an important means of denouncing injustice and lack of freedom. From Israel to Japan, from Manila to Bonn, from Washington to Johannesburg, women with nothing but their silent presence have unmasked what is unjust: "Stop the occupation", "Free our children", "No nuclear testing", "No blood for oil".

They are there. Their wordless presence awakens the conscience of the people, takes sides with the victims, denounces injustices.

This practice has a deep theological meaning in our Judaeo-Christian tradition. In the Hebrew Bible God spoke from within a burning bush to Moses, the leader of an oppressed people, and revealed to him the divine name "Yahweh", "the one who is there" — or as the Jewish theologian Martin Buber translates more accurately, "the one who is present". God says: "I am there for you, on your side. I am going with you, sharing my strength with you." God is the power for life, especially where life is threatened, where the weak need a voice. Women in their silent presence in places of power participate in this divine promise. They represent this quality of God to others with their *being there* for others, for justice and peace and reconciliation. Because they do not shout, they cannot easily be shouted down. The power of this wordless but insistent presence in places where life is violated provokes aggression and police action. But all of this is only proof of the power of silent voices which women cannot afford to lose.

The power of symbolic action

Women have adopted another form of communication inspired by biblical ancestors: they recognize the power of symbolic action. In the peace movement, women have made countless symbolic acts: they have tied roses to the barbed wire of military camps; they have entered into places of danger and planted trees. In our churches people have been bringing well-water for the baptism of their children, to demonstrate that the water which runs from our taps is so often recycled that it has become undrinkable.

Symbolic action does not need many words. It is an offshoot of enforced silence.

Our religious tradition has given us examples and encouragement to communicate with symbolic action. Recall the story of the woman who anointed Jesus on the eve of his trial and death. At a moment of fear and doubt, when his disciples were ready to abandon him and had begun to lose faith in his mission, a woman came and anointed Jesus by pouring precious oil over his head. It was a most affirmative and loving gesture. In the Greek language Jesus was later called *Christos*, "the anointed one".

Jesus was anointed by no one other than this woman in his lifetime. As I understand this story, with her silent gesture she symbolically anointed him to be the suffering Messiah, a messiah other than the one the disciples expected. The language of symbols speaks for itself. Patriarchal theology never looked at this symbolic action as central to Jesus' ministry; it is women's way of discerning which tells us, for it was a woman who anointed Jesus.

From this story we can learn that women have expressed themselves beyond the boundaries of silence imposed on them. In the history of women, symbolic actions are part of their language to speak about God's action and God's justice in the world.

Women speaking — sharing their view of the world

Silence as a way of speaking, symbolic action as silent language — we cannot afford to lose this subversive way of speaking. But today we also have to say that the time of silence is over. Patriarchal theology has stressed Paul's words on the silence of women. But it has not clearly directed our attention to the baptismal formula in which Paul affirms basic equality: "There is no longer Jew or Greek, there is no longer slave or free, there is no longer male and female; for all of you are one in Christ Jesus" (Gal. 3:28). We must take Paul more seriously than patriarchal theology has taken him.

Women learned quickly from experience to overcome patriarchal attitudes. At the end of Paul's theologically important letter to the Romans he commends Phoebe as a deacon or minister. Out of 23 persons mentioned there at least eight are women, not to speak of women in the families referred to; and the first person named is Priscilla, who takes precedence over her husband Aquila.

Today we are overcoming imposed silence in many ways. Women have been called to leadership in the churches. Women are speaking about life-and-death issues on all platforms. Women are discovering the hidden and neglected messages of biblical stories as they read and proclaim the gospel.

As Christian women criticize the oppressive use of holy writings, we are aware that our Christian faith begins with an act of women speaking: the first witnesses of Easter and resurrection were women who dared to speak about a bewildering experience — Christ was not dead but among them with the power of life. But the male disciples considered this to be women's babbling and "an idle tale" (Luke 24:11).

The power of the resurrection was first experienced by women, and this power ended their silence. It opened their way to witness to the power of life over death, the power which changes history. Easter empowered and empowers women to speak about an indestructible way of life. We have discovered that the silencing of women is not the will of God, but the will of patriarchal theology.

Our biblical ancestors like Deborah, Miriam, Mary (in the Magnificat) and the Samaritan woman teach us the uniqueness of women's speaking. But they also teach us that women's speaking can and must have a purpose. God gives us a voice to speak for the voiceless. We have to raise our voices both for our sisters and brothers who are not otherwise listened to and for ourselves. Mary's song, the Magnificat, gives us the direction in which we as women of faith want to develop our voices, not just for the sake of speaking and being heard, but for the sake of a better world in which God's love can be experienced by all God's creatures.

Therefore, women of the world, speak up! Break the silence! Disobey those who teach you to keep silent! Let us unite our voices as instruments of peace, justice and the integrity of creation.

2. A Mujerista *Perspective* on Gospel and Culture

ADA MARIA ISASI-DIAZ

On Good Friday at the church where I worship — in a poor working-class area of New York City called *El Barrio* because of its heavy concentration of Latino peoples — the official service takes place at 3:00 p.m. A group of about eighty persons gathers for this service. After the service several of us women go to Marta's house across the street from the church. Every Good Friday, Marta gets up early and cooks fish. We gather there to eat and talk about what is going on in our lives, all the while waiting for the evening service to start.

The evening service consists of a procession in the neighbourhood with the statue of Mary the Sorrowful Mother, *La Dolorosa*, followed by preaching on "The Seven Sorrows of Mary".[1] Sometimes the priest serving the parish attends this service, but whether or not he does, it is the women of the parish who are in charge of the event. They decide whom to invite to preach, and Angelita, one of their leaders, chooses the four women who will carry the statue of Mary in the procession.

Usually the procession starts with about fifty persons. As we go along, more and more people join. I am always impressed by the mothers holding on to the hands of their younger children. Somehow most of them manage to communicate to the children the importance of this event — an importance that, as some of them have told me, is as much cultural as it is religious. Almost invariably the procession runs into some teenagers. I have repeatedly watched them first laugh at the procession, then grow silent and serious, and eventually fold in and become part of it. Some of them go into the church and some of them do not, but undoubtedly once they overcome the initial embarrassment of doing what the older folks do, they seem to feel right at home in a religious practice that they can identify as specifically belonging to their ethnic community. By the time the procession re-enters the church the number of participants has grown to at least 150.

Having participated for years in this Good Friday evening service and being a Latina myself, I know that this kind of service is often more meaningful to the community than the church services led by the priests. I believe there are three reasons for this. First, when the organizers of an event are part of the people for whom the event is organized, there is greater participation. Second, the great majority (at least 70 percent) of those who participate in church services in *El Barrio* are women. The fact that this evening service centres on a woman, Mary the mother of Jesus, the fact that it recognizes the value of her work, her role in the life of Jesus, and the fact that the women participating in the service can identify with Mary and thus find themselves valued and affirmed — these are reasons for the success of *La Dolorosa*. Third, this service is culture-specific. It does not operate under the false assumption that one can separate gospel from culture, that church services can be the same everywhere. *La Dolorosa* takes into consideration what the people of *El Barrio* really believe about Mary, how they relate to Mary, rather than what the churches say about her and exhort us to believe about her.

As members of a racial-ethnic minority community in the USA, we see our culture threatened every day. We are pressured to lose our ethnic identity and to assimilate ourselves into the dominant white, Anglo-European group.

Christianity is one of the central features of our culture. As women we struggle to preserve our particular incarnation of Christianity, which includes elements from the religions of the indigenous people of America and Africa. But as women struggling for liberation, we know that not all the religious understandings prevalent in our community, no matter from which religious tradition they come, are liberative. Our religious life, as everything else in our lives, exists within a patriarchal framework.

This is why the primary lens through which many of us as Latinas look at religions, the criterion by which we judge what to embrace and what to reject in Christianity, is liberation. We do not believe that elements in today's Christianity which oppress Latinas — such as teachings that insist that women cannot be allowed to offer leadership, oppose the ordination of women or curtail women's ministry even when they are ordained — are indeed part of the gospel message.

Culture

All religious understandings and practices, as everything else in society and in our lives, are part of culture. For me, culture is all that we humans have created to help us to live. Human beings are in need of all kinds of artifacts, which follow necessarily on ideas. And the way we organize ourselves, the way we develop those artifacts and use them, is culture.

Culture is how humans construct reality. There are many different cultures because the situations humans have had to face and continue to face are varied and give rise to many different ways of dealing with them. This is important for us to remember whenever we discuss gospel and culture: *we* construct reality. We as human persons are the ones who decide what things, events, persons ought to mean, what role they ought to play, what values are to govern our lives and our societies.

But the fact is that the reality which has been constructed has been achieved by those who have had the power to do so. We women have not participated in its creation. Yet this reality, created and maintained by those with the power to do so, is projected as natural, as what is and what ought to be.

Since there is no way for us to retrieve the gospel message of Jesus in its "pure" form, and since there is no way to separate the message of Jesus from cultural trappings, religion and the gospel are to a large extent part of the reality that we have constructed to deal with our lives. This is not to deny the importance of belief nor the presence of revealed elements in the gospel message. I am simply pointing out that these revealed gospel elements, our religious beliefs, are not realities apart from culture, apart from the reality humans create in order to be able to survive and live fully.

It is important for us to be very clear that since reality is *constructed*, it can also be changed. This is precisely the struggle in which we are all engaged. All oppressed people are engaged in redefining reality. We are engaged in insisting that the devaluing of woman is not natural, that it is the perspective of patriarchy and that it is wrong. We are saying we cannot accept the elements of our religions that oppress women, even if they are considered essential by those in charge. Religious beliefs and practices that oppress women, even if they are written in the Bible, do not come from God and are not part of God's revelation.

Different readings of the gospel

How do we deal with the cultural variants that result in different readings of the gospel in our churches and communities? How do we as a sisterhood struggling for justice handle our differences? How do we deal with the different ways in which we construct reality, the different ways in which we read the gospel? I believe that a central task of the women's movement today is precisely to learn to deal with differences.

In many areas of the women's movement we have gone from ignoring differences to celebrating differences. To a great extent the time is past when a few women talked in general about women without making clear their own context, without acknowledging the many differences that exist among us, without recognizing that "women" often meant "women from the dominant groups" — thus making women from non-dominant groups all the more invisible. In my part of the world, we are now inclined to *celebrate* differences. But can we jump from ignoring to celebrating differences without *engaging* them? What are we celebrating when women from different racial or ethnic groups have not taken time really to know each other, really to stand in solidarity with each other, really to enable as many of us as possible to participate in the creation of reality?

To be able to say that differences are being engaged, three elements must be present. First, we must recognize, denounce and reject essentialism. We have to give up the often-used principle that "this way — *my way* — of seeing reality is the best (or the only) way". We have to let go of the centre and embrace a plurality of centres, a plurality of ways of seeing reality. I am not in any way denouncing or rejecting specificity. I believe that the specificity claimed and articulated by women belonging to racial or ethnic and other marginalized groups is not the same as essentialism. For me, essentialism is holding on to a specificity that sees itself as unique and normative and discounts the value of all other specificities. In other ways, the essentialism I am denouncing is an insistence on specificity at all cost, which is possible only by those with hegemonic power, the power to impose their views on others without even taking those views into consideration.

Second, if we move from the centre, we do not move to something indefinable or something that is up to each one of us to define. I do not move away from essentialism in order to set myself up as the criterion for judging what is right. Nor on the other hand am I proposing to escape from the "I", which is impossible and undesirable, for in the long run, I am responsible. But denouncing essentialism moves us from the "I" as criterion to an "I" that understands that my perspective is not the only one, that we must constantly redefine what is normative, constantly struggling to find better ways of bringing more and more voices, more and more different women's experiences into consideration when defining what holds us together, what we consider to be good.

Third, in order to engage differences we need to work seriously at the process of values clarification, seeking to articulate even more clearly the criteria for defining what is good for women. From a Christian perspective, this goes hand in hand with clarifying what are the core values of the gospel — not a gospel we dream we can find pure somewhere, but a gospel always incarnated in culture.

The first value we seek is community. We in the USA do not usually call ourselves Latinos or Hispanics, but refer to ourselves as the Latino community or the Hispanic community. In our culture the word *individuo* is used in an almost pejorative sense. An individual is someone who is selfish, egotistical. A person, on the other hand, is someone in relation to others, in relation to community. A person knows and understands that her existence is related to that of others, that we are responsible to others for who we are and what we do.

Community for Latinas not only includes those alive now but extends back in history and forward into the future. Community for us embraces our *abuelitas* (grandmothers) as well as our children. Community is a value, a criterion, that we want to see as part of the norm. Among the many forces opposing community is the competitiveness insisted on and promoted by individualism and capitalism.

A second value is that of justice, which we consider to be an essential — if not *the* essential — element of the gospel message. When we talk about justice we are talking about the distribution of all resources in an equitable way. And we are talking about establishing all the conditions needed to develop one's abilities and having the opportunities needed to be self-determining, to be able really to choose, keeping in mind that in order to choose viable alternatives, real options are needed as well as freedom from coercion.

The third value is peace, in the sense of the Hebrew word *shalom*, which is what the establishment of the "kin-dom" of God is all about.[2] Peace goes well beyond the absence of war and conflict. Peace has to do with fullness of being, fullness of life.

Peace is intrinsically linked to justice, for peace is justice that has triumphed, liberation made reality. Peace means justice at the expense of no one, which requires that we build and maintain a world in which we privilege and repeatedly opt for the poor and the oppressed. Peace means solidarity, listening to the poor and the oppressed and standing shoulder to shoulder with those who continue to struggle for justice.

* * *

In the Latino community in the USA, gospel and culture are intrinsically intertwined. And the lens we use to analyze and value both is a liberative one. Our lives as a minority culture within a hegemonic culture are lives of struggle. But we have learned from our grandmothers, our mothers, our aunts, that we must embrace the struggle for justice and peace, that the struggle gives meaning to our lives, that to be fully alive one has to struggle, that *la vida es la lucha*.[3]

NOTES

[1] The "seven sorrows of Mary" are a combination of events in her life referred to by the gospels and events elaborated by oral tradition. They are: (1) the announcement by Simeon that a sword would pierce Mary's heart (Luke 2:34 35); (2) the flight into Egypt (Matt. 2:13-15); (3) the Child lost and found in the temple (Luke 2:41-51); (4) Mary meeting Jesus on the way to Golgotha; (5) Mary at the foot of the cross (John 19:25-27); (6) Mary receiving the dead body of Jesus; (7) Mary burying Jesus.

[2] The word "kingdom" is both elitist and sexist. We use "kin-dom", which emphasizes the sense of family and community that is so important to us Latinas.

[3] The ideas contained in this essay are more fully developed in my book, *En la Lucha — In the Struggle: Elaborating a* Mujerista *Theology*, Minneapolis, Fortress, 1993.

3. Gospel, Culture and Women in an African-American Context

DELORES S. WILLIAMS

Without the religious moorings supporting it, the word "gospel" simply means "good-news". With those moorings — that is, the Christian tradition which spawned and perpetuates the idea — gospel is a "good-news story" proclaiming salvation brought to humankind through the birth, ministry, death and resurrection of a God-man-child named Jesus of Nazareth. This good-news story is supposed to be powerful enough to continue transforming human character, culture, history and thought throughout the ages. This story is dynamic and alive. It lives in the spirit, moving the human heart to repentance.

However, keepers of the faith in each age must reinterpret this story so that Christians and the world can see and feel and know God's saving grace manifested in their lives, in their time, in their worlds. Thus the good-news has been told differently by different peoples with their different languages, customs, values, myths, symbols and social and economic locations. Culture, then, consists of the languages, myths, symbols, art, values that the various groupings of the human family have developed as the result of living in their different communities for many generations.

Gospel, as good-news and story, comes clad in culture and cannot be separated from it. Thus when Christians missionize they bring the gospel clad in their own culture. And if the motivating political impulse of their culture is imperialism and conquest, the invading gospel meeting an indigenous culture often forces that indigenous culture underground. Or the indigenous culture masks itself so that the invaders do not see its real force.

Claims of the slaveholders' gospel

With this brief treatment of gospel and culture, I turn to my first task in this essay: to show how the African-American community, at one historic moment of its life, rejected an oppressive gospel received from slaveholders and created its own liberating good-news.

The gospel which slaveholders brought to slaves made three basic claims: (1) God ordained and intended the perpetual enslavement of black people; (2) black slaves were therefore to obey their masters; (3) God was totally different from them — black slaves were not in the image of God, and so could not have equality with whites in Christian community.

The slaveholders validated this "gospel" on the basis of biblical stories and texts. They used the story of Ham and Noah to validate their assertion of perpetual slavery for black people. Paul's advice to the slave Onesimus to obey his master "proved" their claim about obedience. Slaveholders advanced the myth of Jesus' white skin and deduced from it that black slaves were outside the image of God. Thus the gospel brought to enslaved Africans by slaveholders was totally clad in the values, beliefs, customs and myths composing the culture of the American slavocracy.

Counteracting this imperialistic cultural intrusion, slaves recounted another gospel, also built on biblical texts and clad in the images, language, values, beliefs and aspirations of their culture. They spoke good-news showing that they were not ordained to obey masters. God was not totally different from them. They were in the image of God, and God reflected their image. They had equality in Christian community.

Let me illustrate this with an African-American folk story, a version of which appears in the *Book of Negro Folklore* by Langston Hughes and Arna Bontemps. The story, which no doubt dates back to the slave era in the United States, was told by the folks in this way:

> One day Jesus looked up at the sky and saw it was going to be a pretty day. He said to his disciples, "I'm gonna walk and talk with y'all today. Everybody get a piece of rock and put it in yo pocket." All the disciples, except Peter, got a nice piece of rock and put it in they pocket. Peter got a little bitta' rock not much bigger than a pebble and put it in his pocket. Jesus walked and talked with them disciples for a long time. Then they come to a

river. Jesus said, "Let's us stop and rest." Then he dipped into the river and got a mess of fish. They cooked the fish and Jesus said, "Now take dose rock out a' yo pockets 'cause I'm gonna turn them into bread and y'all can make some fish sandmiches." Everybody's bread was big enough for a fish sandmich except Peter's. He had a terrible time tryin' to wrap that little scrap of bread around that fish! Jesus walked and talked with them disciples until night fall.

The next day Jesus looked up at the sky and saw it was going to be another pretty day. He said to the disciples, "I'm gonna walk and talk with y'all again today. Everybody get a piece of rock and put it in yo pocket." All the disciples, except Peter, got a nice size rock and put it in they pockets. Peter went and tore down one side of a mountain and dragged it along, always lagging behind the others. They got to the river and Jesus said "Y'all, let's rest!" Peter still lagging behind. When Peter finally got to the river, Jesus said, "Why Peter, that's a mighty fine piece of rock you got there! I'm gonna build my church on that rock!" Peter said, "Naw you ain't neither! You gonna' turn this rock into bread!" Jesus saw Peter meant that thing. So he took the other disciples' rocks and pieced them together. The church is built on them little rocks Jesus pieced together.

To the slave, the good-news in all this is that Jesus lived in the world as they did. He was subject to the ways of nature: he appreciated a "pretty day". The story does not project the miraculous "Peace! Be still!" motif of the New Testament story in which Jesus used these words to calm a turbulent sea. In the language of slave culture, Jesus has been transported into the thick of slave existence, and his miraculous power manifests itself in a custom of black culinary art: making fish "sandmiches". This kind of power expressed in relation to the ordinary suggests an ancient African-American Christian belief — that God helps the needy to make a way out of no way, for example by turning stone to bread. The folk story indicates that God brings unity to the scattered constituents of creation, including slaves. Thus Jesus makes the church out of many pieces of difference. The folk use their cultural mask of humour to hide an image of God that was radical for their time. This God is at home with folk culture and is thoroughly clothed in their humanity. This is a God-Master whom Peter does not obey — a God who has respect for human intention and chooses another way to accomplish God's own intention, a God who achieves unity out of a heterogeneous grouping rather than a homogeneous mass.

The point to be underscored here is that slaves, like the slave-masters, used the Bible to tell another version of good-news which included them and was shaped by their culture rather than the culture of the slavocracy. They merged two different events in the biblical story of Jesus' ministry — Jesus' feeding the multitude with a few loaves and fishes and his words to Peter "on this rock I will build my church" — to communicate a compelling message relevant to us today: that God communicates with us in the rhythm of our daily lives orchestrated by the instruments of our various cultures.

An oppressive cultural translation

At another moment of history, however, some African-Americans told the gospel in a way which was oppressive for women, even though the telling gave hope to the community. This brings me to my second task: to demonstrate how this same method of cultural translation by black Americans became oppressive gospel when doctrine and male dominance guided the method of presentation. I begin with another story.

The scene is a black Baptist church in the southern USA in the late 1940s or early 1950s. The minister — tall and handsome, with a deep, resonant voice — guides the congregation through the ritual to start Sunday morning services. He is standing at the pulpit. The choir, white-robed, is behind him. He booms forth this question: "Who do you say God is?" The choir responds, "God of God, King of Kings, Father everlasting!" The preacher poses the question again: "Who do you say God is?" A small woman, a domestic worker, comes to the front of the church and answers: "Poor little Mary's boy, and they nailed him to a tree, and they nailed him to a tree!" The preacher asks again: "Who do you say God is?" The choir responds, "God of God, King of Kings, Father everlasting!" Again he asks the question, and again the small domestic worker responds: "Poor little Mary's boy, and she laid him in the grave, and she laid him in the grave." "Who do you say God is?" the preacher repeats. "God of God, King of Kings, Father everlasting," the choir responds. For the last time the preacher bellows out the question: "Who do you say God is?" The domestic worker responds: "Poor little Mary's boy, and he got up from the dead, and he got up from the dead!" By this time the congregation is electric because many had family members who had either gotten up or were trying to get up from the death of poverty, substance abuse, racism, domestic violence.

With this ritual, the preacher brought the good-news of hope into the community using the African-American cultural pattern of call and response. The message of hope was "getting up from the dead". The oppressive part for women was the omission of "little Mary's *daughters*" from the equation. How were they getting up from the dead? Who was caring for and about black women's bodies amid the many crucifixions they suffered? Beneath the words and images of the choir, the preacher and the domestic worker was a theological suggestion of a doctrine of a trinity in which father, king and son came together in one dominant assertion of male power. While the "good-news" in this ritual excluded and therefore oppressed women, it also provided hope for a community of mothers needing to believe that one day their children would rise up from whatever death was holding them. And the emphasis on Mary's suffering son by one of the poor among them brought the community's issues of poverty and innocent suffering into the presentation of the good-news. Along with the call-and-response pattern, this reinforced the African-American Christian community's sense of religious identity grounded in the innocent death and suffering of Jesus. At this particular time, many innocent black people were being lynched by white hate groups like the Ku Klux Klan.

Black women themselves redeemed the good-news from the oppression indicated by their exclusion from vital worship processes in the African-American Christian community. At a later moment in the community's life, womanist theologians and scholars uncovered the deposits of black women's culture and discovered a rich history of resistance. They found Christian foremothers shaping a culture of resistance, telling the good-news of black women's faith that, as their piety and politics came together in the struggle against their oppression, God was by their side.

Women's history, gospel and culture

This brings me to my third and final task: to show how uncovering the history and culture of African-American women not only brings a liberating character to the good-news for women, but provides insights that can help women from diverse cultures build solidarity.

The cultural deposits of this history of resistance have shown that the relation of black women to biblical personalities differed from those which the male-dominated Christian cultures (black or white) had always lifted up as models of courage. These biblical figures were female, and among them were Hagar and Jezebel. Sexist and racist forces in the dominant Anglo-American culture had maligned Jezebel, stigmatizing her as a deviate, as a vamp whose characteristics were modelled in American society by black women. Nevertheless, the stories of these two women in the Bible paralleled the life experience of African-American women and showed two different results of women's resistance activity with which African-American women were familiar. Black women who, like Hagar, suffered the cruelty of slavery and ran away from slavery also believed, like Hagar, that they experienced God's gift of new vision to see resources for survival where they had seen none before. Like Jezebel, many black women worked and plotted against powerful forces in order to support black nationalistic efforts in the United States. Some of these black women were lynched for their efforts — utterly destroyed as Jezebel was for her nationalistic efforts.

Out of this history of female resistance have come certain cultural values which black women have tried to pass along from generation to generation. An example of this is the advice about how to resist violence which a slave mother gave her daughter. In the daughter's words, "She [the mother] did not make a good slave. She was too high-spirited and independent. The one doctrine of my mother's teaching which was branded upon my senses was that I should never let anyone abuse me." The heart of the black woman's doctrine of resistance was this: "Fight, and if you can't fight, kick. If you can't kick, then bite."[1]

Yet in the culture of black women's resistance, "fight" could mean something quite nonviolent. It could mean alliance politics like those demonstrated by Harriet Tubman as she single-handedly liberated hundreds of slaves. She made alliances with abolition forces, underground railroad conductors and others in order to accomplish her goal of liberation. Jane Lewis used silent and subtle strategies as she rowed a boat in the midnight hours back and forth between the Indiana and Kentucky shores of the Ohio River to pick up runaway slaves and take them to free territory. Milla Granson, a slave, used the same kind of silence and subtlety as she secretly taught many slaves to read and write. Some of them forged passes and slipped away into Canada.

This is not to suggest that black women's resistance in the United States has been one long history of nonviolent activity. There were, during slave time, cases of infanticide when slave mothers killed their children to keep them from becoming slaves. There was the case in 1776 of Maria, a slave in Roxbury, Massachusetts, who was sentenced to death by burning on a charge of incendiarism. In Kentucky, a slave woman was given the death sentence for mixing an ounce of powdered glass with gravy that she meant to serve to her master and mistress. Two women, Lucy and Charlotte, were active in the slave revolt led by Nat Turner in Virginia in 1831.

This attention given to the resistance history and culture of African-American women has led some black female Christian theologians to challenge and reinterpret some of the foundations of the Christian religion laid by theological doctrine. They have expressed these challenges using the content of African-American women's culture. Supported by what I identify as African women's surrogacy experience, I have challenged the ways in which Christians have been taught to understand redemption as Jesus on the cross in the place of sinful humankind. Some womanist theologians are asking whether acceptance of substitution theories of atonement by black women can lead them to be passive in the face of their own oppression. Using the African cultural notion of the spirit coming into human life by mounting the human body, some womanists raise questions about the Christian way of identifying incarnation with Jesus. They suggest that the incarnation happened first with Mary the mother of Jesus. As the spirit mounted Mary, the Word first became flesh in her body. Thus women's bodies become an important subject in discussions about incarnational theology. Christology has also been reinterpreted by womanist theologians to suggest that we consider Christ as a black woman if we, like liberation theologians, identify Christ in our time with the poorest of the poor in our society, the most oppressed of the oppressed, who are black women.

African-American womanist theologians have thus made Christian communities aware of the possibility of new understandings of the foundations of the religion engendered by reinterpretation of the gospel within the context of African-American women's history and culture of resistance. This way of presenting the good-news through the instruments of

African-American women's culture has yielded insights that may be useful to women of different cultures trying to achieve solidarity. Let me conclude by mentioning three of these insights:
— Women sharing information about the strategies they use and have used to construct "women-friendly" gospel and culture.
— Women dialoguing with each other cross-culturally not only about the resistance strategies they have developed to transform oppressive Christian symbols, doctrines and practices, but also communicating to each other the stories of their faith — how their piety and politics work together to sustain the struggle for justice.
— Women committed to a new gospel, believing that God is now saying to the church: "Women are the rock upon which I now build my church." Women believing that the task of rebuilding the church actually involves reconstructing the church. Women committed to sharing information cross-culturally about how this is to be done.

NOTE

[1] For a full discussion of this, see my book *Sisters in the Wilderness: The Challenge of Womanist God-Talk*, Maryknoll NY, Orbis, 1993, pp.136-39.

4. Rereading the Bible as a Latin American Black Woman

SILVIA REGINA DE LIMA

What has the rereading of the Bible from the viewpoint of Latin American black women meant?

The Bible in the life of communities in Latin America

Rereading the Bible has given the community of the poor in Latin America and the Caribbean a source of strength and affirmation in their struggle for dignity. The Bible is a place of encounter with the God of life and an instrument of liberation. What we mean by a popular rereading of the Bible is the appropriation of the Word by the poor.

This rereading is marked by a series of breaks with tradition. The first is a *political* break, which recognizes the poor as interpreters in their own right. The place of encounter with the word is the life of the poorest, understood in the broadest sense as the worker, the peasant, the indigenous person, the black person, the woman — the popular milieu in general.

A second break, resulting from this, is a *spiritual* break. The encounter with the poor leads to the encounter with God, who reveals him/herself in the world of the poor. This gives rise to a new spirituality inspired by compassion, kindness and solidarity with the poor, as an expression of God's preferential love for the least among us.

This in turn leads to the third break, the *hermeneutical* break. The emergence and affirmation of new "hermeneutical subjects" and the recognition of a hermeneutic of liberation spell conflict with the oppressive hermeneutics that typify the predominant theories of biblical interpretation. This confronts us with the struggle for the reappropriation of the meaning of the word.

The Latin American feminist rereading gives expression to this process of breaking with tradition. It is a process of deconstruction and rediscovery of the meaning of the Bible.

Stages in the process

As Elsa Tamez has observed, one stage does not necessarily imply the completion of the preceding one. In everyday life, in the life of communities, in the lives of women, these different stages co-exist. The discovery of women as the poorest of the poor marks the first stage in the feminist rereading in Latin America. This is part and parcel of the thinking of liberation theology. The popular movements, the demands, the political struggles in which women are involved encourage them to reread the Bible with eyes that seek a God who affirms them in their struggle and quest for life for their peoples and communities. Bible studies seek to revisit and bring out the importance of characters such as Deborah, Esther and Mary as leaders and bearers of the message of life and liberation in history.

In the second stage, women turn to the Bible to find God's feminine dimensions. They develop a special sensitivity for detecting the presence or absence, the visibility or invisibility, the silence in regard to women in biblical passages. They refuse to conform to the patriarchy present in theological discourse. God is father, but also mother. The shortcoming of this stage is its persistence in an erroneous vision of the female and male identities. It continues to associate femininity exclusively with fragility, affection and tenderness. The female-male relationship is seen as complementary in nature, and there is no criticism of the historical-cultural construction of the social roles of the man and the woman.

The third stage is marked by the search for an holistic theology and a rereading guided by the multiple relations in which women live out their lives. The rigid and essentialist patterns of understanding the feminine and the masculine are questioned, and proposals are made for evolving beyond them. This step represents an epistemological break, as it proposes a different way of conceiving identities, of knowing, of relating to the world, to persons and to the divinity. The rereading of the Bible is oriented towards breaking with old paradigms for understanding the world and humankind. Dialogue based on differences assumes major importance. A strongly emerging theme is that of cultures and the existing differences among women themselves. This is the stage of encounter with diversity.

Five criteria

This Latin American black feminist rereading is taking place in the light of diversity, bringing into a dialogue black culture, the experience of women and the Christian message. It is being carried forward by Christian women, based on the encounter with a black culture, specifically with elements of traditional African religions. The experience of living out the Christian faith and embracing the ancestral religions with love and faith is a practice common to black men and women in Christian communities in Brazil. While this practice has been part of the history of black people since their arrival in Latin America and the Caribbean, in recent years it has been the place of encounter with a new face of God, which is an important element in the endeavours of different groups to recover black identity and black dignity.

Among the new perspectives and approaches emerging from this black feminist rereading of the Bible, we may discern five criteria:

1. The daily lives of black women as the place of encounter with God. The historical context of the life of black women is their struggle for survival. There are many single women who shoulder the responsibility for both their life and the lives of their children. The God of the survivors manifests him/herself concretely in the challenges of each day. For centuries, this God has been consolation in the face of affliction, company and tenderness in solitude, strength in combat. God's accompaniment and support is daily strength that makes the impossible possible. It is a God-experience in the form of succour in time of need. God is health in the form of blessing, herbal teas and baths; God is food that is shared on feast days or with a neighbour in times of need. We ask God for money and that we never lack work. No matter what name we give to God, no matter how we address ourselves to

God, this is the God of the poorest, who calls them to a life of dignity.

2. God has our face; God reveals God's self in the history of black people. When we talk about a God who reveals him/herself in history, we are referring to the specific history of persons. For the black community these stories of revelation enable us to salvage the memory, the past that many would wish to forget. Recovering the memory is appropriating history and liberating oneself on its basis. The God who accompanied black women in their triumphs and sufferings does not always correspond to the God traditionally confessed in Christian churches. Often the imposition of Christianity led to the concealment of the God who in fact answered their cries and shouts. Both this God in history and this history of God in life confirm that we do not need to stop being black, nor to deny our bodies, our past, the religious experience of our forebears in order to serve and please the God of Christianity.

3. The rereading of the Bible is a meeting of histories and traditions. Rereading the Bible entails a reinterpretation of our past, of the history of our forebears. This reinterpretation of history gives us an idea of God's revelation in biblical history and the keys to understanding and recognizing it. For us women, God has two histories of liberation and continues to act and to be revealed by these different paths. In either heritage we find both elements that justify the subordination of women and principles that shore up our dignity. It is only the profound personal experience of our faith and culture and our day-to-day courage and resolve as black women that enable us to assess critically what may or may not be a liberating God-experience.

4. Revelation and culture — concealing and revealing God. History has taught us that God manifested him/herself in a culture. The transposition of this God-experience to other peoples and cultures and its imposition on them led to the hiding, the concealment of God. God no longer meant life and liberation but death and domination. To restore the dynamic of God's revelation, it is necessary to consider the freedom of the Spirit. The Spirit goes before us: it is wind, it is air, it circulates and causes life to be reborn. In this sense, we may say that the experience of the encounter with God in ancestral religions has made it possible to liberate God from the narrow concepts to which Western Christianity reduced God. This has made it possible for us to encounter a God who is closer to nature, who places us in communion with the cosmos, a God who speaks to us through the utterances of wise women, a God who makes community with the poorest of the poor, who dances in our body, who plays and eats at feasts.

5. *The rereading of the Bible demands a rereading of the Bible as a whole.* These ideas challenge us to reread the Bible as a whole, not only taking the passages that speak of the liberation of women, but also turning to the Bible to find a God who transcends the exclusive, sexist and racist images that were transmitted to us. This exercise also means recognizing the cultural and historic limits of the biblical context, and the inputs, richness and revelations of God in nonbiblical cultures.

An affirmation

We black women can affirm that we believe in a God who is Life-Creativeness, Liberating-Diversity. Hence, the reinterpretation of the Bible and of history makes it possible for us to have that loving encounter with God, who accompanies and supports us along the way. Our liberation is also the liberation from the many images of God that have justified and still justify the sexist and racist structures of society. With these eyes, with our whole body, with our histories, we are drawing closer together to enjoy the never-ending newness that is God.

5. The Wisdom of Mothers Knows No Boundaries

CHUNG HYUN-KYUNG

The story of Jihe

A few years ago there was a poor woman living with her mother and son in a small province in Korea. Let us call her Jihe, which means "wisdom" in Korean. Jihe may have been a single mother, because the story makes no mention of a husband. Being a poor single mother is perhaps the lowest position for a woman in the hierarchical society in Korea.

One day when Jihe's son was playing ball in the street, laughing and running, he was hit by a car and killed instantly. The driver of the car was a powerful politician in the province. The accident was clearly his fault but he refused to take responsibility for it. Since he had a great deal of influence with the police in the province, he managed to avoid any charges. Jihe and her mother cried and cried, holding the cold, bloody body of their boy. But no one seemed to hear their cries. There was no justice for these two poor women.

Some time later the politician ran for congress. The dead boy's grandmother was so angry that she produced leaflets and distributed them at his nominating convention, charging the politician with his crime. The politician responded by suing the grandmother for libel. Of course, the powerless grandmother lost the case because the trial was corrupt, and she was imprisoned.

In anger and despair, Jihe nearly went out of her mind. But after many days of crying and sighing, she determined to take revenge in her own way. In a worldly sense she had nothing — no money, no education, no husband, no political power, no advocate. Yet her dead son and her imprisoned mother were present in her dreams and pushed her to right the wrong.

Jihe pulled herself together. She was determined to fight for justice no matter what! In her humble house she made an altar. There she put portraits of the politician, the police chief, the judge and the politician's lawyer, which she drew with her own hand.

Every morning in front of a bowl of pure water, she prayed for justice to all the deities she knew: Ha-Na-Nim (the traditional Korean supreme God), Kwan-Woon Chang-Nim (the warrior God of Korean Shamanism), Ye-Su-Nim (Jesus Christ). Jihe prayed with all her heart, body and soul. Then she shot through each portrait with a bow and arrow saying, "O compassionate God of justice, let them be punished."

The rumour of her prayer and action began to spread all over the province. In Korean cultural belief, if someone curses you for one hundred days you will soon be dead. Finally, the politician who had hurt Jihe became very frightened, because in the Korean shamanistic tradition her ritual would lead to his death. In order to stop this spiritual energy directed against him, the man had Jihe's mother released from prison, acknowledged his fault and compensated Jihe financially for her son's death.

When I first heard this story, my heart leaped with joy and discovery. It sounds both very ancient and very contemporary to me. It seems like the paradigmatic story of Korean women's spirituality. This is a story of the kind we as Korean women have all known, but never owned as a symbol of Korean women's power. Of course, the majority of my theological teachers have not used this kind of story as a main source for theological work.

Asian Christian mission history

There are reasons why Jihe's victorious experience of struggle cannot be the main source of Korean and many other Asian theologies.

Jihe's voice is absent because most Asian churches have been mission churches. Our theological work, Christian education and church organization have been shaped by the ultimate "missionary position", in which Western Christianity, culture and theological paradigms are always on top and our Asian religions, cultures and spiritual paradigms are always underneath. No other positions were allowed, especially in early mission history. In this context, there is no room for authentic theological articulation by people of the third world, by Asians, by women.

Certain scholars have suggested that there are three different ways of understanding the encounter between Christianity and other religions and cultures of the world: exclusivism, inclusivism and pluralism. Exclusivism is the most common position of many Asian churches and their theologies. This model is based on the exclusive truth claim of Christianity. According to this position there is no salvation outside the Christian church; and on the basis of this understanding many of our Christian brothers and sisters have defied our cultures, traditional religions and rituals in order to be "real, pure, good" Christians.

Inclusivism is a more enlightened position than exclusivism. Some progressive Asian churches, even though they are minorities in Asia, discern revelatory truths and values in our traditional cultures and religions. This position appreciates our traditional religions and cultures, but only to the point that the supremacy of salvation by Christ is not threatened. In this circle, the talk of inculturation, indigenization, contextualization flourishes. Some call our Buddhist brothers and sisters, living a life of compassion and wisdom, "anonymous Christians". Others liken the relation between our traditional religions and cultures and Christianity to that between the Old Testament and the New Testament. In this inclusivist position, however, only Christ fulfils and consummates every shortcoming of other religions.

The third position — pluralism — is followed by a minority of Asian churches and theologians. They accept that there is salvation in other religions and try to respect other religions while keeping their Christian identity clear. Pluralism is the most enlightened position among the three in relation to other religions, respecting differences and living side by side with differences.

When I reflect on the above three positions, I feel that none of them can contain my theological struggle and that of some of my Asian sisters. The exclusivist and inclusivist models are still very imperialistic, reflecting the past colonial attitudes of the West to the East, while the pluralistic model is too academic, Western and male. It is too academic because it treats the different religions as neatly arranged entities in clearly marked categories labelled Buddhism, Christianity, Shamanism, Confucianism and the like. But this form of pluralism, in which the separate categories are distinct and do not cross one another's boundaries, exists only in academia. When I look at the popular religiosity of Asian women, the religions do not exist in that neat way under these name tags. There is a messy and fluid process of cross-permeation among the different religions.

This neatly separated pluralism can be observed in some Western societies, where the presence of Buddhism, Islam, Hinduism or any other major world religion except Christianity is still recent. Each religious group lives separately in its sect without transforming the mainline religion of the society, which is Christianity.

I think this neatly separated pluralism is for male-centred institutional religions, because maintaining purity of doctrine has been the centre of their concern. But when I look at everyday life-based women's cosmic spirituality in Asia, it is clear that what matters is not doctrinal purity, but what is liberating, what is healing, what is life-giving. Therefore the word "pluralism" as used in academia cannot really describe Asian women's religiosity.

Let me make this clearer by sharing my own experience within the Korean context. When people ask me how I define my religiosity, I say, "My bowels are shamanist, my heart is Buddhist, my right brain is Confucianist, my left brain is Christian and my public-speaking language is Christian language." This means that I am a Christian who lives out the reality, power and dangers of the Buddhist, shamanist and Confucian traditions which are alive in my people's history.

If religiosity is one of the thickest layers of people's collective memory in any culture, the very thickest layer of the collective memory might, for me, be Shamanism. The history of Shamanism in Korea is more than five thousand years old. That of Buddhism goes back more than two thousand years and that of Confucianism about seven hundred years. In contrast, Protestant Christianity in Korea is only about one hundred years old.

If the newly discussed biological theory that acquired characteristics can be inherited is correct, I can claim to have inherited Buddhist, shamanist and Confucian genes in every cell of my body. In other words, I was born with a shamanist, Buddhist and Confucian inclination or ethos. But even if we do not accept this biological theory, we can still claim that we inherit our ancient religions through our languages, thought-forms and symbols, because they are an intrinsic part of our culture. In this sense, we are not living in the neatly arranged pluralism of Western academia, but are living out different religions within ourselves. Many of us from Asia know this experience. It is like living with a "community of gods" or "continuum of divinity" in the "family of religions".

What is happening here is not an inter-religious dialogue in the context of neatly arranged and separated pluralism. Rather it is an *intra*-religious dialogue, taking place within ourselves. This community of gods and family of religions are within us. That is why any serious Asian person needs archaeological exploration of many layers of spiritual self and community.

Sometimes this community of gods and family of religions works like traditional Asian medicine jars. If you go to an Asian herbal doctor, you will be impressed by many different boxes of herbs for healing. As the Asian doctor uses specific herbs for specific diseases, we call on a specific god for specific problems and questions. For example, I could not find any cure for my impossible love life in the Christian religion. Through my five years of feminist psychotherapy and Zen Buddhist meditation and with the help of the Taoist-shamanist ritual of letting go, which I carried out with my mother, I finally came to be at peace with my love life. Or sometimes it works like a kaleidoscope, creating highly sophisticated combinations of colours and shapes in order to show us visions for survival and liberation. In this community of gods, one enhances the presence of another when they interact with a dynamic synergy that vivifies and deepens the meaning of our lives.

What name can I give to this reality? This is more than pluralism. In my book *Struggle to be the Sun Again*, I call this reality "survival liberation-centred syncretism". Especially when I observe popular religiosity among Asian women, the expression "survival liberation-centred syncretism" or "life-centred syncretism" seems to convey aptly the religious reality of the people.

Syncretism has of course been a dangerous and dirty word for many Christian theologians in the West. Their vehement rejection of syncretism seems to me to be an admission of their ignorance of the history of religions as well as an admission of their theological imperialism.

In Asian women's popular religiosity there are many "fusions of horizons", and a very subtle, highly sophisticated, continuously improvised synergetic dance of gods and religions, as was seen in the story of poor mother Jihe. What mattered for her was not doctrinal purity, but her survival and liberation.

New eyes on gospel and "culture"

When I reflect on the gospel and culture debate in ecumenical circles on the basis of this life-experience, it seems to me that many traditional gospel and culture models and "Christ and culture" debates are bankrupt. In these models, gospel and Christ are always connected with acting seed, sperm, yeast and living water, and our cultures and religions are considered as possible soil, baby-basket, dough and container. It seems that Western missions have Christ and the gospel and we Asians have religion and culture. This dualism is based on a narcissistic fantasy of Western cultural imperialism, not on reality. We need a new model for a "relationship between gospel and culture" which is not based on the dualism between gospel and culture, because we receive gospel as a cultural form and we also discover gospel in our own culture. Therefore we have to learn how to talk about gospel as culture and culture as gospel.

We should also look critically at our social location when we talk about gospel and culture. Which gospel and whose culture do we want to combine? Certainly I do not want to integrate the gospel of triumphalistic, post-Constantinian, imperial-type Christianity, which is tainted with colonialism, capitalism, patriarchy and Texas-style fundamentalism, with our feudalistic, patriarchal, militaristic culture. Rather I want to see the birth of a new Christianity in Asia which comes out of the love-making between the stories of the community of Jesus and the stories of our people. The name of this newborn baby will be a living Asian Christianity.

Asian women's spirituality and Asian women's theology

Doing theology with this self-awareness of being Asians living with a community of gods and family of religion within ourselves implies a radical paradigm shift in Asian theology. So far, the generation of my teachers, whom I would describe as first-generation Asian liberation theologians, are trying to adjust their body language and body rhythms to the language of Christianity. But my generation, whom I call second-generation Asian liberation theologians, are trying to adjust Christian public language to our body language, our primordial bodily rhythm.

Without this shift, we are headed for either madness and perpetual schizophrenia of identity (always looking at ourselves with alien criteria) or self-alienation. We will function well but never be in touch with our true selves, our sources of power and our ancient memories. We have to say yes to this original stirring, delight, primordial rhythm of our ancient body and wild power of organic spirituality for our survival and liberation.

When I am fully aware of this body language, I can envision the direction of the future of Asian women's theology.
— We will have a shift in the area of authority in doing theology. We will claim that we are the text and that the Bible and church traditions are our context.
— Theology will move from being a Christocentric Christian theology to being a creation- or life-centred Christian theology.
— Our theological audiences will move from the basic Christian community to the basic human community and finally to the basic community of all beings, past, present and future, living and dead.
— Our theological emphasis will move from one-sided *kenosis* to a balance between *kenosis* and *theosis*.
— Our passion for connection with our neighbours will move from inter-religious dialogue to inter-religious praxis for liberation.
— Our main data for theology will come from the popular religiosity of Asian grassroots women rather than from the organized institutions of Asia, as we heard from Jihe's story.

* * *

There are many hidden Jihes in Asia. They have been there from ancient times to the present. They have continuously selected the life-giving power in this continuum of divinity. This spirituality has been somewhat messy, dark, moist, warm and wild. It is spirituality from the womb of becoming, the metamorphosis of life.

I hope all of us will remember that place in our people's spirituality, recover our body language, and finally transform public language and the structure of "he-story", the story of death-wishing, power-hungry, virginity-obsessed patriarchs.

6. Gospel and Cultures in Africa: Through Women's Eyes

MERCY AMBA ODUYOYE

Given the many facets of the title of this essay, I must begin by defining my focus with some degree of precision. In this attempt to present the subject of "gospel and cultures" as African women see it — or, to be more accurate, as one African woman sees it — the women represented are Christian women, women who "go to church" and take the Christian religion seriously, and who could be said to have developed African Christian women's cultures. I use the plural form "cultures" because among Christian women there is a diverse multiplicity of accommodations of Christianity and African cultures.

Second, although Africa is a vast continent, it should not be carved up according to imposed criteria like colonial boundaries, European languages, the Sahara or the predominance of the Christian or Islamic religion. At the same time generalizations about Africa often lead to misleading conclusions and unhelpful actions. The discourse presented here is located specifically among the Akan of Ghana; but to highlight the commonalities of African culture, the illustrations range freely, reflecting the commonalities that one can label — in the singular — as African culture.

Our third preliminary consideration is the description of what culture comprises. The broad understanding I work with is that whatever is not nature is culture. Culture is what human beings and human communities have created to make the earth a habitat for communities of human beings. This broad definition of culture is necessary because Africa has a religious culture: the whole way of life evolves out of and around religious beliefs. Here the relevant religious factor is Africa's cosmic religion, which places a great premium on relationships. All that exists derives from and relates to God. The natural world, the spirit world and the human community are all inter-related, and communication among them is the norm of existence. The human family in this visible and dynamic dimension we call life and those in the spirit world, the other dimension (the dead and the unborn), constitute a continuum. Hence in African culture, family, community and religious practices are of primary importance.

Since culture is human creation it evolves and changes. We must therefore locate our discussion in the contemporary culture that is being shaped and experienced in Africa. A brief overview is appropriate at this point.

The European invasion which began in the 15th century and reached its height in the 19th did not leave Africa unaffected. The religious element of this cultural contact was a Christianity that had learned haughtiness from the Roman emperors; its mercantile element was a colonialism that had learned greed and exploitation from European feudalism. The messianic stance of its carriers made the whole enterprise altogether ethnocentric and later simply racist. European military power and duplicity turned Africa into an annex that fed Europe with wealth. The humanity of the African was simply denied and obliterated. Those who resisted were marginalized or eliminated. The result is an Africa whose bowels have been plucked out and the space filled with chaff, a continent that has exchanged compassion for callousness, a sense of community for allegiance with the wealthy.

Africa today has a culture of genocidal war and conflict that kills and displaces many people. Africa has a culture of poverty imposed and maintained by complex factors. Africa is developing a culture of silencing potentially liberating voices. Africa's culture is moving from communalism into elitism. Africa is evolving a culture of much good talk and little liberative action.

It is against this background that we review our subject of gospel and cultures. This contribution aims at stimulating discussion on the following:
— what counts as good news in Africa;
— the essentials of the Christian gospel;
— the points of contact between the indigenous cultures and the incoming culture of Euro-American Christianity;
— what African women count as good news;

— how women participate in creating gospel-based culture;
— the gospel and solidarity among women of diverse cultures.

Good news

The word "gospel" is the English equivalent of the Greek word *evangelion*, meaning "good news". The opening sentence of Mark's "gospel" — his record of the Christ-event — is: "The beginning of the good news of Jesus Christ, the Son of God" (Mark 1:1). A familiar theological question asks, *Is* Jesus the good news, or did Jesus *bring* the good news? In Luke's account of the gospel we meet Jesus, a Galilean carpenter, in his home town Nazareth, explaining himself to the townspeople and telling them what the good news comprises by quoting to them from their own scriptures and tradition. Isaiah 61 provided a summary of good news as being what the poor, the vulnerable and dehumanized need to hear and to experience. The gospel is the power that generates liberation. It is the announcement of God's jubilee year. Another writer telling the story of Jesus reports him as saying, "I came that they may have life, and have it abundantly" (John 10:10). All four gospels speak of good news. Matthew does not describe or define it, but he suggests that the announced name of Mary's baby is itself good news: that God is with us. This is what Jesus told his disciples to keep in mind and to tell all: Emmanuel — God with us.

What is the vision of a community that lives as though God is indeed with us? What we read of the Jesus story confirms that Jesus was a person of good news. The story is good news because it is life-giving and liberative, energizing all who hear it to act for or against it. No one can be neutral. Jesus gave his life for the good news because what is not life-giving is bad news. The biblical creation story tells of a God who creates what is good, the good news of making chaos beautiful. The Christian tradition says Jesus was in the beginning with God as all this good was being brought into being. So the gospel of Jesus ought to have elements to enable us to transform our contemporary chaos into a multidimensional, variegated beauty that we can celebrate together.

Good news in Africa is what reconstructs the continent, its people and structures so that they approximate the beauty God calls good. As in many other parts of Africa, Akan culture has normative descriptions of the good life. Common to all Africans is the love of life, the sacredness of life and the centrality of community, which operates in concentric but porous circles with God at the centre of it all. Material prosperity is sought while materialism is decried. A strong link is maintained with the natural world, which is also seen as God-originated and therefore sacred. Africans take the spirit world seriously and maintain constant rapport with it through the religion and ethics that regulate their community life.

Good news in Africa is all that responds to this vision of "the good life". The gospel of Jesus Christ coincides at many points with the African vision of life. Many Africans recognized the religion of Jesus and became Christians in spite of the negative social, economic and political relations between them and the Euro-Americans who brought the continent Christianity, commerce, colonialism and racism. The essentials of the Christian gospel were good news to African ears.

Good news of the gospel

In a world of poverty and privation, Jesus never minimized people's need for sustenance for their body and healing from their diseases. The gospel is good news for those who love life. The gospel values of care for the weak and vulnerable, justice for the exploited and compassion for the suffering are good news. The Magnificat, the Beatitudes, the ten commandments and Psalm 23 crystallize the gospel for many who occupy the pews of African churches, and the majority are women.

The fact that love of God and of neighbour is central to the religion of Jesus is good news. For Africans who take the spirit world seriously it is good to keep in mind that all spirits are accountable to God the source, the one Jesus is said to have called "Father".

Aspects of the Christ-event have sometimes been interpreted in ways that serve life-denying purposes. The simplicity of the life of Jesus and that of his followers, his teaching about nonviolence and love of the enemy and his acceptance of the cross have been used in this way, while the elements of justice, compassion, sharing, validating the being and skills of all humanity, inclusiveness, empowerment and celebration of the other have been singularly absent in the churches' version of the good news of Jesus Christ. The good news has suffered from human cultures of androcentrism and patriarchy.

Official church theology, teaching and preaching often spell bad news for Africans. For most women in Africa this means bearing the double burden of the oppressive aspects of both African culture and church teachings.

Dealing with gospel and culture, one is tempted to separate the gospel of Jesus Christ from the church in Africa, and Christianity from the human institutions called churches. But such an exercise would be futile, as the essential question is how people's lives are shaped by and who contributes to the Christian culture that the churches in Africa wish to promote among their adherents. A gospel culture challenges both the church culture and the African culture.

Cardinal points of contact

The interaction of gospel and African culture has contributed to the evolving cultures in Africa. Taking the example of Ghana, one can observe elements of both mutual affirmation and challenge between the life-giving and life-sustaining culture that conforms to the religion and life-style of Jesus which we have called "gospel culture" on the one side and African culture on the other. The gospel demands a caring community; so does the African culture. Today neither church nor society in Africa is very caring. The gospel demands justice and equality in human relations, respect for the other and the environment, and the structuring of community and building of relationships that create well-being and a just peace on this earth. The gospel challenges both the church and society to a transformation that will turn human cultures into gospel culture.

As far as women are concerned, the gospel culture critiques both church and society for creating or condoning injustice to women. It demands that churches stand in solidarity with women as they struggle to be rid of endemic patriarchy. Where patriarchal ideology marginalizes women, the church has reinforced that ideology by its own marginalization of women or counselling them to patience and self-sacrifice. Simply put, patriarchy is an ideology that validates lording it over "the other" and ignoring justice for the vulnerable.

The gospel culture challenges both church and society for their trivializing of the humanity of women. African men and women who are comfortable in their present existence are tempted to make a selective use of cultural demands and provisions, according to which "African culture" becomes an alibi for maintaining the inequalities of the status quo. The same goes for the Christian culture which chooses to validate the oppressive aspects of African culture. In such situations the liberative elements of the gospel are hidden away. A gospel culture is one that unveils and highlights the good news and makes it operative.

Women and church culture

The liberative perspectives brought by the gospel of Jesus Christ are capable of transforming both church culture and African culture. For the most part, however, both African culture and church culture appear as stumbling-blocks to putting into effect the ethic that derives from the gospel of Jesus Christ. The Akan say, "All human beings are children of God"; cultural practices seem to add the rider, "but women are less so." In church we hear the scripture that says

"All human beings are created in the image of God"; church practices and teachings seem to say, "but women are less so." The agenda of church and society does not flow from the *credenda*. There is a split of faith from life which the religion of Jesus and gospel culture challenges.

There is more than ample evidence that cultural attitudes influence and bias the one-sided theology of the church and, in Africa, prevent the church from having an empowering critical voice on African culture. When it is not silent and dissociated from cultural critique, the church actually reinforces and perpetuates injustices against women. The church culture is itself oppressive. The women who have internalized it glory in being "good women", while women who challenge it by the standards of the gospel culture are calumniated and marginalized even further.

Much of the injustice done to African women centres on the meaning and purpose of marriage, marital relations and household codes. Marriage gifts or securities which have become "bride price" play a key role in these relationships and understandings. Speaking on planned parenthood, a Zambian Christian man remarks: "The cows I gave as the bride price for my son's wife are producing calves, so the bride ought to be producing children." That a wife might be compared to cows reflects the reality that wives are often counted among a man's property. This leads to levirate marriage and the "property-grabbing" to which widows are subjected. Although the church culture does not put it so crudely, the language of the marriage ceremony in most churches strengthens the perception that the woman is a junior partner in the marriage, reinforcing legal provisions and traditional attitudes that make a woman a perpetual minor who cannot own property in her own right.

If human beings are stewards of the earth, then women too have the responsibility to "own" and till the land. In a recent discussion of land rights in one African country, the head of state is reported to have asked, "Why do women want land?" This economic injustice, coupled with notions of religious pollution, make some women revisit the Bible and especially the religion of Jesus to learn who they are. They have taken it upon themselves to challenge the uncritical appropriation of traditional culture. Their stance is that women and men together must struggle to see the evolution of a gospel culture. What pollutes human beings and the earth are greed and injustice, not our bodily functions, which we have learned to manage.

For women who prepared themselves for the UN Conference on Women and the NGO Forum in Beijing, the revolution that happened among Chinese women almost half a century ago was an inspiration. They read and heard that "during the long night of pre-revolutionary China, the broad masses of Chinese women, oppressed by the 'three big mountains' (imperialism, feudalism and bureaucratic capitalism) and bound by the 'four ropes' (political power, clan power, religious authority and authority of husband) subsisted at society's lowest levels. They allowed themselves to be ordered about and were subject to endless oppression, bullying and humiliation."[1] Traditionally the "mountains" were called obediences and the "ropes" virtues. The language is itself significant: ropes that bind one to the wheel of oppression should not be called virtues, and no one should obey that which is life-denying.

In Beijing the world's women declared their intention no longer to "allow themselves to be ordered about". On this rests global women's solidarity. For Christian women the strength to resist, challenge, reconstruct and transform comes from the gospel. The strategy of the NGO Forum "Seeing the World through Women's Eyes" does not suggest that *all* women see things in the same way. Yet from Beijing one comes away impressed by the similarities in vision and the determination to see a world transformed. It is with this in mind that we take another look at how African women appropriate the gospel culture for the critique and transformation of both church culture and African culture.

Three responses and two actors

African women select the empowering, liberating elements of received Christianity. They appropriate what is life-affirming in African culture to augment and enrich the gospel culture. They are women whose life-style is directed by a critical appropriation of religion and culture. They are not afraid to let go of that which is life-denying and that which is not life-enhancing.

A second response is typified by church women who believe that all Christian women should conform to an image of the "good woman" sculpted from the late 19th- and early 20th-century models represented by the wives of the Euro-American missionaries and women teachers. They are comfortable defining themselves by who their husbands are and maintaining the household codes of the New Testament epistles; and they would not hesitate to silence any woman who dared to want to speak in church. A woman should rock cradles, not boats.

A third type of response is a critical appreciation and appropriation of both the received culture and the received religion. This would challenge the gospel culture of patience under suffering in cases where the suffering is not salvific or where it is required only of women. This response works for the reconstruction of the damaged image of God in women, for resistance to the embedded life-denying forces and for the transformation of human community in conformity with the tenets of the good news of Jesus Christ.

The actors in this respect are many. Here we focus attention on two emphases that have emerged since 1989: educators and researchers whose focus is women in theology and women's development. Educators and researchers in Africa used to be Europeans or North Americans or Africans (most of them men) schooled in Euro-American norms of scholarship. Today a new paradigm is in operation. Creating awareness and getting women to come to a critical understanding of the lives they live has become the passion of many African women.

Specifically church-based operations include women involved in laity formation and women who stimulate women's participation in churches and ecumenical bodies. They are many and have been at it for a long while, but what has emanated from the women's desk of the All Africa Conference of Churches since its Togo conference in 1989 is most remarkable. Programmes of "economic literacy" that demystify economics and enable women to develop a critical consciousness towards oppressive systems like "economic structural adjustment programmes" are making women more articulate about their lives and their participation in history-making. Women's programmes on violence against women are forcing the churches in Africa to reflect on what they require of women. These efforts are revealing much that is debilitating in both the received church culture and the indigenous African culture.

The strategy of these educators is clear: provide the opportunity for women to hear themselves speak directly about their lives; move them to an analysis of these experiences; prod them to judge their experiences by the measure of human dignity and the gospel affirmation of fullness of life. Many if not all will inevitably move towards concrete actions that will transform death into life, enhance what is life-giving and engender the resurrection of the true humanity of women. Examples of this methodology are being shared with the global sisterhood and the wider church through videos.

Parallel to this, the Circle of Concerned African Women Theologians, inaugurated in 1989 in Accra, has undertaken to run institutes on "African women in religion and culture". The origins of the Circle are in the 1975 UN international year and the liberative community of the Ecumenical Association of Third World Theologians (EATWOT). It took a long time to come into existence because before 1976 African women theologians were a rare species. The concern is to research, write and publish on African women in religion and culture in order to break the silence surrounding women's lives and to challenge church culture and African culture to begin a journey towards transformation.

Women of the Circle engage in research and hold educational events to unveil the oppressive aspects of cultures and highlight their empowering elements for appropriation. They reflect theologically on women's lives and use a mutually empowering participatory model of research. The Circle is ecumenical and multireligious. Some of its members are pastors, others are theological teachers, but many come from other disciplines as well.

Women and the gospel

Women associated with the two movements described above will have no more to do with the uncritical use of Bible and cultural norms: they are doing much rereading of both. They are empowered by "the strong women" of the Bible including those of the so-called apocryphal writings. They go before authorities with the courage of Esther and defend their bodies and challenge lying rapists in the spirit of Susanna. They are learning to deal with the rape of Tamar and the murder of Jephthah's nameless daughter. For many are the African women who have been sacrificed on the altar of the honour and wishes and vows of men.

Jesus is a special friend of African Christian women. The words of Mary in the Magnificat are the hermeneutical tool for interpreting the Christ-event, for indeed, as the story is told, it is a woman who made Jesus of Nazareth *christos*, the anointed one. The rest of the Bible and liturgies and ethical teachings of the churches are all put through the sieve of justice, compassion, empowering, caring community — all that makes up the gospel culture.

For African Christian women, the Bible remains a comforting presence. It says "God is with us", and that is the good news. Gospel culture evolves where people relate to one another and to the environment as persons who live in the presence of God.

What African women propose, then, is that we go beyond juxtaposing gospel and cultures. We propose a move towards "gospel culture": a way of life creatively crafted from the humanizing elements of African culture and church culture. If the Christian gospel is good news, then there is much in our cultures that it should challenge and much in African culture that it could absorb to augment and enhance its transforming powers. "Gospel culture" will evolve when we are rid of all that negates fullness of life and blasphemes against the image of God in humanity.

NOTE

[1] *China in Brief: Protection of Chinese Women's Rights and Interests*, Beijing, New Star Press, 1993, p.1.

7. "Seeing the World through Women's Eyes"

OFELIA ORTEGA

Seeing the world through women's eyes — that is what happened at Beijing. It was an exhilarating, liberating, challenging experience.

We saw together — thirty thousand of us — the world of cultures, oppressive and liberating. We arrived in Beijing full of expectations and hope. The preparatory meetings of the NGO Forum were not easy. We had concerns about the location, transportation, visas, accommodation and the like; nevertheless, we were inspired by the great commitment of the women from the China Christian Council during the preparatory process and in the Beijing gathering itself. We met a wonderful group of Chinese women with a deep understanding of their Christian testimony in church and society.

The settling-in process of the "Ecumenical Women United" group (formed by the World Council of Churches, Lutheran World Federation, World Federation of Methodist Women, World Union of Catholic Women, World Alliance of Reformed Churches, World Vision International and World Student Christian Federation) was partly frustrated due to logistical problems. We were situated in a very small tent at one end of the campus, not at all easy to find, which made it more difficult for us to offer a space of Christian hospitality in Huairou.

Nevertheless, Ecumenical Women United offered five panel conversations in a large, adequate room on the broad theme "Women of faith who respond...", and five biblical studies on "Let the Spirit flow". The World Council of Churches facilitated the presence at the NGO Forum of some fifty women from around the world and, together with staff, these women animated a series of WCC workshops on economy, racism, health and the challenge of HIV/AIDS; young women for a violence-free world; gospel, cultures and women; and networking for action in solidarity with migrant women.

Once on campus, we realized that no matter what space the institutional structures give to women, we were able to expand ourselves in surprising ways.

We Christian women were everywhere — in the workshops organized by Ecumenical Women United, in the youth and regional tents, gathering information at communication and press offices, in plenaries, marching, talking, eating, laughing, dancing, praying with 30,000 other women. It was a terrific experience! It showed us that it is not possible to put boundaries on the women's movement today.

A life-liberating movement

The women's movement, like the human rights and ecological movements, is one of the contemporary life-liberating movements, affirming the ethnic and cultural identities of oppressed groups and fostering religious expressions that can resist systemic powers. Christian women around the world have also come to struggle in the face of systematic and prolonged oppression. Cultures have played a key role in perpetuating such oppression.

Therefore it is very important to develop a religious cultural analysis from a women's perspective in order to determine what is good and life-giving for women.

A religious cultural analysis must include:
— critiques of cultures from within those cultures, from the perspective of women's daily reality;
— critiques of dominant cultures from the cultures of the dominated;
— analysis of women's struggles, in order to keep alive the cultural memories that empower women and make it possible for them to maintain their self-identity;
— cultural study of fundamentalist ideas that present a totalizing view of life and reality often used to control and disempower women;
— recognition of the fact that there is not only one truth, because the revelation of God happens in different ways in different cultures. [1]

We discovered in Beijing how religion and cultural symbols are being rediscovered — reinvented, in some instances — for the struggle. These symbols help us to develop a spirituality for life that is sustained by the vision of justice, self-determination and well-being for all of creation.

It is clear that when women started the feminist movement, they were acting against injustice and discrimination. It is indeed a life-liberating movement.

Women have unmasked gender bias as one of the primary causes of poverty, because in its various forms it prevents hundreds of millions of women from obtaining the education, training, health service, child care and legal status needed to escape from poverty.

Equality, equity and liberation (the indivisible elements of justice) are growing through the action of women's movements. Women are searching for *the common good* rather than only the good of men.

At the same time, we as women recognize that all cultures perpetuate certain patriarchal institutions of discrimination against women. For this reason we see the need for the transformation of cultures, challenged by the gospel, so that cultural hermeneutics can become an interpretative tool for women in their feminist theological search. Cultural hermeneutics can open our eyes to possibilities that might move us to different commitments.[2]

Two other emphases characterize the women's movement as a life-liberating movement. First, women see the need to assert the liberation potential within all cultures, because the dominant Western culture has so often attempted to suppress cultures and impose values and ways of life on peoples of the South that it becomes an imperative to value the seeds of freedom and authenticity in each culture.

At the same time it is necessary to say that if culture is to be liberating, it must be rooted in the real lives of women, and both women's and men's experiences must be seen as integral to local cultures.

Cultural analysis must be done from a gender perspective in order to challenge the violence perpetuated against women daily with claims of the culture's supremacy or the inviolability of justice and gender or, more importantly, of the gospel.

This will guide us to the second emphasis: to see the urgency of the "dialogue of cultures" that must permeate the new visions of the ecumenical movement for the next century. We need to dialogue with each other cross-culturally, not only to share information about resistance strategies but also to communicate to each other the stories of faith that have sustained us in our struggle for justice.

Our workshop in Beijing helped us to reflect on what we women of the Judaeo-Christian tradition have learned in the past decades as part of the worldwide women's movement. And the reports of the team visits undertaken to mark the midpoint of the World Council of Churches' Ecumenical Decade of Churches in Solidarity with Women have told of the incredible power in women, how deeply they love the church and how ready they are to commit themselves to working in the church and their society.

NOTES

[1] See the report on the Intercontinental Meeting of EATWOT Women, Coronado, Costa Rica, December 1994.
[2] See Musimbi Kanyoro, "Cultural Hermeneutics: An African Contribution", in Ofelia Ortega, ed., *Women's Visions: Theological Reflection, Celebration, Action*, Geneva, WCC Publications, 1995, pp.18-29.

Contributors

Jean Stromberg was assistant to the WCC's general secretary from 1988 to 1992. She is currently director of the WCC's New York office.

Bärbel von Wartenberg-Potter was director of the Sub-unit on Women in Church and Society of the WCC from 1980 to 1985. She is general secretary elect of the Council of Christian Churches in Germany.

Ada Maria Isasi-Diaz is professor of feminist Hispanic theology, Drew University, Madison, NJ, USA.

Delores S. Williams is Paul Tillich professor of theology and culture, Union Theological Seminary, New York, USA.

Silvia Regina de Lima is professor of biblical studies at the Latin American Biblical Seminary, San José, Costa Rica.

Chung Hyun-Kyung is associate professor of ecumenical studies at Union Theological Seminary, New York, USA.

Mercy Amba Oduyoye from Ghana was deputy general secretary of the WCC from 1987 to 1994. She is coordinator of the Circle of Concerned African Women Theologians.

Ofelia Ortega is an executive secretary in ecumenical theological education with the WCC's Programme Unit I, Unity and Renewal.